Women are from Venus

Women are from Venus

Understanding the
Woman in Your Life

John Gray

Thorsons

Thorsons
An Imprint of HarperCollins*Publishers*
77–85 Fulham Palace Road,
Hammersmith, London W6 8JB

The Thorsons website address is:
www.Thorsons.com

Material taken from *Men are From Mars, Women are
From Venus*, originally published in the USA by
HarperCollins*Publishers*, published by Thorsons 1993
This revised edition published by Thorsons 1999

1 3 5 7 9 10 8 6 4 2

© John Gray 1992

John Gray asserts the moral right to
be identified as the author of this work

A catalogue record for this book
is available from the British Library

ISBN 0 7225 3954 1

Printed and bound in Great Britain by
Caledonian International Book Manufacturing Ltd, Glasgow

Women are from Venus

Introduction

A relationship holds many challenges. Once we have overcome these we can grow together in love.

A relationship is like a garden: it must be nurtured each day for it to grow into something wonderful.

♡ *Women are from Venus* ♡

Imagine that men are from Mars and women are from Venus. One day long ago the Martians, looking through their telescopes, discovered the Venusians. They fell in love and quickly invented space travel and flew to Venus. The Venusians welcomed the Martians with open arms. The love between the Venusians and Martians was magical.

Though from different worlds, they revelled in their differences and spent months learning about each other, exploring and appreciating their different needs.

Then they decided to fly to Earth. But the Martians and the Venusians forgot they were from different planets and since that day men and women have been in conflict.

♡ *Women are from Venus* ♡

Life on Venus

On Venus, everyone studies psychology and has at least a Master's degree in counselling.

Women tend to be more involved in personal growth, spirituality, and everything that can nurture life, healing and growth.

Venusians are very intuitive.

The Need to Feel Special

A woman loves the romance of receiving flowers, small presents and spontaneous gestures of affection.

When a man gives a woman flowers
or sends her love notes, he lets her
know that she is special.

～

*They are symbols of love that make
her feel beautiful and feminine.*

～

♡ *The Need to Feel Special* ♡

When a man regularly brings romance into the relationship it makes a woman feel cherished and reminds her not to give so much.

A man thrives on appreciation so it is important for a woman to catch him doing something helpful and thank him for it.

Men and women often express their love differently. It is difficult for a woman to believe that a man who forgets her birthdays or anniversaries could really love her.

♡ *The Need to Feel Special* ♡

A woman is motivated and empowered when she feels cherished.

♡ *The Need to Feel Special* ♡

A woman never gets bored of hearing a man say, 'I love you'. It allows her to feel his love.

A woman likes to receive constant reassurance that she is loved. Many men mistakenly think that once they have laid the groundwork in the relationship, then she should know from then on that she is loved.

Before a woman can feel a passion
for sex, she needs to feel loved,
cherished and romanced.

♡ *The Need to Feel Special* ♡

For women, flirting is like shopping. When she shops she is deciding what she likes and doesn't like. When she is flirting she is saying, 'I am looking and liking what I see. Maybe you could be the one to make me happy'.

♡ *The Need to Feel Special* ♡

~

*A woman feels physical chemistry
after she has felt mental and
emotional chemistry.*

~

A woman loves it when a man wants to touch her or hold her hand.

She doesn't feel loved if the only time he wants to connect in this way is when he wants sex.

♡ The Need to Feel Special ♡

A man needs to pay attention to romantic details that will please a woman and help relieve her of the pressure of caring for others. This allows her to open up and feel her sexual desire.

A woman can want to have sex as much as a man. The difference is that she needs to feel satisfied in love before she can feel a strong desire for sex.

A man needs to be aware that when a woman is unsure about having sex, it means she needs time, attention and tender communication. Once he realises this he can overcome his natural tendency to feel rejected.

♡ *The Need to Feel Special* ♡

An orgasm is not the goal in sex for a woman. She can enjoy the intimacy, passion and affection just as much.

Women want to be equal partners in a relationship. They don't want to be the one calling all the shots and are turned off by passive and submissive men.

A woman can initiate a relationship by giving a brief look that says 'you could be the one to make me happy'. In this subtle way she actually motivates a man to start a relationship.

However, once she is in a relationship, a woman may forget how important it is to still give that message to
him and neglect to send it.

When a woman senses a man's confidence, she feels reassured. It allows her to relax and know that she will get what she needs.

When she feels that she is number one in a man's life then, quite easily, she admires him.

A woman thrives when she feels adored and special.

When She Wants to Talk

When a woman becomes upset or stressed by her day, to find relief, she seeks out someone she trusts and talks in great detail.

A woman does not prioritize the significance of any problems. If she is upset, then she is upset about it all, big and small.

To feel better, a woman talks about past problems, future problems, potential problems, even problems that have no solution.

The more talk and exploration, the better she feels.

A woman feels good about herself when she has loving friends with whom to share her feelings and problems.

*A woman expects a man to open
up and talk about his problems the
way that she does.*

But a man does not speak about his problems in the same way and she can resent him for not being more open.

A woman is not ashamed of having problems. Her ego is dependent not on looking 'competent' but rather on being in loving relationships.

Better Communication

The only time a woman is silent is when what she has to say would be hurtful or when she no longer wants to talk to a man because she doesn't trust him.

~

When a man is silent it is easy
for a woman to imagine the worst.

~

♡ Better Communication ♡

Good communication is essential for a woman. It is difficult for her to feel loving and tender feelings without it.

A woman uses communication to explore her feelings, organize her thoughts and clarify her priorities.

Men often do not realize that an emotional woman is not inflexible in her thinking. She does not talk to express fixed opinions, but to explore her range of feelings.

When a woman communicates she
is not just sharing information
but also herself.

♡ Better Communication ♡

A woman's feelings are less about the outer world and more about how she experiences the outer world.

A man needs to realize that when a woman talks about her feelings she is not suggesting that her feelings are fact. He need not argue or get defensive.

A woman decides what course of action to take by exploring her feelings out loud. She does not necessarily always speak to make a point.

When telling her story, a woman enjoys letting the suspense build because it brings more feeling to it. Other women appreciate this build-up, while men rarely do – they want the important facts.

To fully express her feelings, a woman can assume poetic license to use various superlatives, metaphors and generalisations.

When a woman has a problem, she needs to make it clear that she does not want a solution. This makes it easier for a man to switch from the 'fixing' mode to the 'hearing' mode.

When a man responds to a woman's troubles with sympathy and not solutions, he makes her feel loved and nurtured.

Women feel nurtured when a man initiates a conversation. It shows that he is interested in what she has to share and she need not fear she is boring him.

A man should give a woman 20 minutes of unsolicited, quality attention – he shouldn't read the newspaper or get distracted by anything.

If a man is worried or upset, a woman mistakenly thinks that by asking a lot of questions or being a good listener, this will make him feel better.

When a woman listens to someone, she will continue to reassure the speaker that she is listening and that she cares. She instinctively wants to support others in the way that she would want to be supported.

For good communication a man should sometimes touch his partner with his hand. He should show interest in what she does during the day, in the books she reads and in the people she relates to. When listening to her he should reassure her that he is interested by making little noises like 'aha', 'uh-huh' or 'hmmmm'.

Work And Stress

Men and women react to stress differently. She needs closeness and understanding while he often needs to be alone.

When a woman is suffering from stress she often feels that she can't cope with all the jobs that need to be done.

At work, women give as much as men do. The difference is that when they get home they continue to give.

Most women see their home as a haven from the outside world. This means that even if they have had a hard day and they want to rest and relax, they can't until the home is in order.

When a woman is at work, she detaches herself from her emotional needs. Once she returns home she needs the loving support of her partner.

At work a woman is goal-driven. By being non-goal-orientated at home she can nurture her feminine side.

A man often mistakenly thinks that when they become more financially secure as a couple, his partner will become happier. He needs to be aware that once her physical needs have been met, she will feel her emotional needs more.

Her Emotional Life

A woman doesn't like it when a man expects her to be more detached. It makes her feel like it is wrong or weak to have feelings.

A woman doesn't like a man's condescending attitude when she asks questions about a decision that he needs to make. It makes her feel like she is a burden or that she is wasting his time.

A woman doesn't like it when a man raises his voice or maintains dogmatically that he is right. It makes her feel like she is wrong and that he doesn't care about her point of view.

When a woman is frustrated by poor communication she will often feel the only way to be heard is to express disagreement.

A woman tends to be more aware than a man about their relationship needs and problems. A man often acts as if everything is fine which makes the woman feel as if she is asking for too much and he will never do anything to change.

When a problem or conflict arises, a woman often takes responsibility and the blame for it. She will look at all the different ways she could have acted to produce a different result.

There are few things more damaging to a woman than negative self-talk. She is denying herself the power to take control and create more of her life.

Worrying for others is one way a woman expresses her love and caring. For her, being happy when the person you love is upset just doesn't seem right.

The most common way a woman will unknowingly start an argument is by asking rhetorical questions and thereby communicating a message of disapproval.

A woman will say, 'I'm sorry' as a way to say, 'I care about what you are feeling'. It doesn't mean she is apologizing for doing something wrong.

A woman may use concern and worry as a way of avoiding the painful feelings of anger, guilt, fear or disappointment.

A woman may use a whole host of positive emotions like hope and happiness as a way of covering up her painful feelings.

Her Hurt is Not Always His Fault

A woman is like a wave. When she feels loved her self-esteem rises to a crest in a wave motion.

Her mood may change suddenly and her wave crashes down. This crash is usually temporary. After her feelings have reached a trough, her mood will shift and she will feel good about herself again. Automatically her wave begins to rise back up.

When a woman's wave rises she feels she has an abundance of love to give.

When it falls she feels her inner emptiness and needs to be filled up with love.

When she hits bottom it is time for emotional housecleaning.

A man should always remember that once a woman lets her hurt or anger out, she will feel much better.

～

When a woman gets angry or upset she is not necessarily passing blame.

～

♡ *Her Hurt is Not Always His Fault* ♡

The last thing a woman appreciates when her mood is getting worse is someone telling her why she shouldn't be down.

Sometimes when a woman is hurting she may even agree intellectually that she shouldn't be hurting. But this does not affect how she is feeling – she needs to work through it.

♡ *Her Hurt is Not Always His Fault* ♡

Whenever her feelings have been hurt, a man should give her sympathy and say to her, 'I'm sorry you feel hurt'. Then he should be silent and let her feel his understanding of her hurt.

♡ *Her Hurt is Not Always His Fault* ♡

*It is a mistake to offer solutions
or explanations of why her hurt
is not his fault.*

♡ *Her Hurt is Not Always His Fault* ♡

A woman will pull away when she doesn't trust another to understand her feelings, when she has been hurt or when someone has done something wrong and disappointed her.

If a woman has pulled away, becoming intimate again requires a period of reacquaintance. She may need more time to regain the same level of intimacy.

When a woman trusts, she becomes more open and receptive. The more her need to be heard and understood is fulfilled, the easier it is for her to give her partner the acceptance he needs and deserves.

When She Feels Rejected

If a woman has a family history of rejection, then a man needs to be aware that she will be more sensitive to feelings of abandonment.

Women feel insecure when a man pulls away. She needs to know that he will be back, so even the words, 'Let's talk about it later', can help reassure her.

Rejection, judgement and abandonment can be most painful for some woman because deep inside their unconscious they may hold the incorrect belief that they are unworthy of receiving more.

Women might portray themselves as perfect in an attempt to convince themselves that they are worthy of love.

A woman is particularly vulnerable to the negative and incorrect belief that she doesn't deserve to be loved. Because she is afraid of not being supported, she unknowingly pushes away the support she needs.

A woman may take the blame and assume responsibility for whatever is upsetting a man rather than argue. She will end up losing herself in the long run.

To avoid feeling hurt in a confrontation, a woman sometimes puts a smile on her face and appears to be happy with everything.

She may even fool herself and believe that everything is fine thereby sacrificing or denying her wants.

Trying to Change Him

A woman needs to be aware that if she tries to change a man, he will feel controlled, manipulated and unloved.

It is a natural tendency for a woman to try to change herself on a conscious level. If she tries to change a man he will rebel and possibly reject her.

When a man refuses to change, a woman feels that he doesn't love her enough. In fact, he feels that he is not loved enough.

A sign of great love for a woman is to offer help and assistance without being asked. Offering constructive criticism is an act of love.

♡ *Trying to Change Him* ♡

A woman firmly believes that when something is working – it can always work better.

Her nature is to want to improve things.

If a man resists a woman's suggestions she feels as though he doesn't care – and she feels he is not respecting her.

A woman can unknowingly annoy a man by offering seemingly harmless advice, for example:

"Don't put that there. It will get lost"
"You should call a plumber. He'll know
    what to do"
"Why are we waiting for a table?
    Didn't you make a reservation?"
"You're driving too fast. Slow down or
    you'll get a ticket"

♡ Trying to Change Him ♡

A Woman's Needs

Many women deny their needs
from a fear of appearing needy.

♡ *A Woman's Needs* ♡

Even if a woman feels her needs are not being met, it is a big mistake for her to stop expressing what she wants and start doing everything herself.

It is important that a woman learns
how to express her needs and desires
without demanding or blaming.

♡ *A Woman's Needs* ♡

Many women are over-giving in a relationship. When they realize this they often close the door, not giving their partner the chance to change.

A woman needs to believe that she deserves to be loved. Once she realizes this she opens the door for her partner to give and love her more.

Many women today are tired of giving and not receiving love in return. They want time off. Time to explore being themselves. Time to care about themselves first.

In her younger years, a woman is much more willing to sacrifice and mould herself to fulfil her partner's needs.

A woman has the uncanny ability to give happily until the score is about thirty to zero. When she gives with a smile on her face, it doesn't necessarily mean that the score is close to even.

A woman gives as much as she can and only notices that she has received less when she is empty and spent.

She will often agree to do what her partner wants, but that doesn't mean that is what she wants.

She doesn't start out keeping score; she gives freely and assumes that he will do the same.

When a woman keeps score, the little things are just as important as the big things, so a single rose gets as many points as paying the rent on time.

A woman will have a hidden feeling that says, 'I don't want to tell him what I need; if he really loves me he will know'.

Both men and women should remember that their partners do not always automatically know what they want.

A woman doesn't like it when a man forgets to do the things she asks so that she ends up sounding like a nag. She feels like she is then begging for his support.

♡ *A Woman's Needs* ♡

She needs to feel respected and remembered. Instead she feels neglected and at the bottom of his priority list.